Ghetto Love

Renaissance

By

Sedelia Gardner

Avid Readers Publishing Group

Lakewood, California

Ghetto Love: Renaissance

Avid Readers Publishing Group

http://www.avidreaderspg.com

ISBN-13: 978-1-61286-250-7

Printed in the United States

Renaissance simply means to be re-born. I cannot forget or try to hide the writings that I had published before now. Because that is how I got started . And after time God took that talent and used it so that He could be praised.

The meaning of Ghetto –

1- It means someone has no class or is very loud and obnoxious.

2- If it's a racial situation, it could also be used to describe a black person.

3- A ghetto can be a place where poor people live the slums of the city

4- **If it is the latter, the person is probably finding cheap ways to do things.**

The meaning of Love –

1- Love is a feeling that really can't be described.

2- It's something you can only feel.

3- It's about caring for someone deeply, and never wanting to let go.

4- It's about thinking about them constantly.

Now that you have read the meaning of the words maybe you can understand why I chose the title Ghetto Love for my poetry book series. It is very simple. I needed to even in my lowest place find a cheap way to show some love to God. The love I have for God cannot be described and if I had all the money in the world I still wouldn't be able to show Him enough. Ghetto Love!

This book is dedicated to my prayer circle members Sherri Coleman, Sharon Poole, Lenny West, Zoltan Murry, Gladys Polk, Al-Shariyfa Robinson, Kyle Wenokur, Karen Williams, Jessica Perez, Renee Gomez, Anthony Edwards, Hal Norrils, Phyllis Remo, Angelita Aguilar, Annie Warren, Iva Hines, Monetta Harrison and Calinda Lucas.

And Minister Kenesia Mouton and my phone line sisters of prayer. I don't know everyone's name on the prayer line but your prayers have been such a big inspiration to this book.

Thank you Lord for giving me a chance to praise you and uplift your name and to show others that I am grateful for what you have done for me. I may not be dancing in the streets showing my love for You but I am doing it with the talent you blessed me with and using it to the best of my ability to give you praise.

This poetry series is a brief description of some of the things that I had to go through, experience and overcome in order to find God and my faith. It is easy to talk about anything but it is hard to be unique about your talking. This book like the others I have written also has one of my signature poems in the shape of a glass. Enjoy!

Proverbs 12:14

Wise words bring many benefits, and hard work brings rewards!

Wash me

Here I am standing here before you

With a tattered dirty white robe

And a dark but forgivable past

Here I am

Asking you to wash me

Here I am standing here before you

I have traveled my long dark journey

But I found you in the mist of my travels

Now I am asking you to wash me

Here I am

With the tears falling from my eyes

And my heart is crying out for mercy

Asking you to wash me

Sedelia Gardner

Unleashed

Let me loosen up my buttons

And pop my collar open

So I can unleash this praise in my soul

That I've been holding in for so long

It's time to lift my hands up in the air

And give glory to the most High

Let me loosen up my buttons

And pop my collar open

So I can unleash these tears in my eyes

That I've been holding back for so long

It's time to let them flow

As I give praise to the most High

Let me loosen up my buttons

And pop my collar open

So I can unleash this spirit of worship

That I've been holding in for so long

It's time to let it go

And give it all to the most High

Sedelia Gardner

Tears

Every tear that fell

From my eye

God knew its story

Every tear that fell

From my eye

God knew its pain

Every tear that fell

From my eye

God gathered in His hands

Every tear that fell

From my eye

God returned it to back to me as a blessing

Sedelia Gardner

Blue Hair Lady

Blue haired lady I see you

Taking your place upon the front church pew

Your hair looks like pure silver

Glistening in the morning sun

But when I see it

I see a shade of blue

Blue haired lady

So fancy is your Sunday hat

Your silver hair shining on this Sunday morning

Were you up late washing your pretty silver hair?

But can still see

A shade of blue

Blue haired lady

I see you holding your Bible close to you

Instead of praying for others you're

Praying to God that He never

Opens your closet door

Ghetto Love: Renaissance

No matter what the hair dresser does

Don't look down at me

I can still see a shade of blue

Sedelia Gardner

Wings of an Angel

The wings of an Angel

Is what I am holding on to

As they slide me over valleys

And glide me over troubled waters

Untouched I am

And not a feather lost

On the wings of an Angel

I am carried high in the skies

And placed on the mountain top

To get my rest

On the wings of an Angel

Where the softness

Gives me comfort and rest

The victory is ours

And not a feather lost

Sedelia Gardner

Ghetto Love: Renaissance

I

I never would have made it

Without you I never would

Have been made whole

Without you so let the

Blood pour down on

Me Lord and

Always

Cover

Me

N

O

W

A

N

D

Forever

Sedelia Gardner

Sometimes

Sometimes I just have

To bow my head

Say a prayer

And weather the storm

Not because I am weak

But because I have

Given it to You

Sometimes I just have

To kneel down

Say a prayer

And let the tears flow

Not because I am weak

But because I need

Mercy from You

Sometimes I just have

To stop fighting

Say a prayer

And be still

Not because I am weak

But because I have

Victory in You

Sedelia Gardner

Back Church Pew

There I sit on the back church pew

Trying to hide my eyes

From the pastor's stare

I hear his words

Like he has written his sermon

Just for me

On the back church pew

The wood is worn down

But it is the strongest

Pew in the church

There we gather

Like there is nowhere else

For us to go

Even thou there are empty

Pews up front

There we sit hanging our heads low

Leaning on one another

Ghetto Love: Renaissance

For a silent touch of comfort

Does anyone even know

Of the burdens you are holding up

Back church pew

Sedelia Gardner

Hitch Hiker

You pick me up a hitchhiker on the side of the road

I was just a lonely traveler going down a long dark road

You opened up your door

And You let me come in

Never asked me where I was going

And didn't ask me where I had been

I closed my eyes to get some rest

And You took over

And placed me back on the same path

The scenery looks different to me

Now that I am riding down this road with You

I once was a lonely hitchhiker

Until I found You

Sedelia Gardner

I Stand Up

My back keeps hurting

Because I know people

Are talking behind it

I don't even worry about it

I stand up

So God can continue on blessing me

I stand up

My back keeps on aching

Because I know people

Are stabbing me in it

I don't even cry about it

I stand up

So God can keep on blessing me

I stand up

My back is tired

Because I know people

Are loading burdens on me

I don't even fight about it

I stand up

So God can continue on blessing me

Sedelia Gardner

I Have A Rock

I have a rock in me

I am so glad

You were able to work

In a place

People couldn't see

I have a rock in me

I am so glad

That I only looked bad

For a short moment to

People who could see

I have a rock in me

I am so glad

That rock made me ready

To face the things

People couldn't see

Sedelia Gardner

How Precious

How precious

Is your robe

That the touch

Of the hem

Made a woman whole

How precious

Is your touch

That it made

That blind man see

How precious

Are your words

That when spoken

Rose the dead

How precious

Is your blood

That was spilled

To save us all

Sedelia Gardner

Strong

Where is my mother

Who nurse me from her breast?

Where is my father

Who is the head of the household?

Where is my sister

Has she ran and hid

Where is my brother

Who said he would protect me

There is no one left here

That my eyes can see

Where are my friends

Who said they would never leave me

Where is my love

Who said till death do us part

Where are my children

Are they scared to show their faces?

Grandma, grandpa, aunts, uncles and cousins

Sedelia Gardner

No trace of them found

I never knew how strong I was

Until all I had left was God

Sedelia Gardner

Diamond

A small rock is found

Looks like someone has found a diamond

It is washed off

And cut into perfection

After perfection is reached

It is placed in a perfect setting

For all to adore its flawless beauty

The light comes down from above

And shines through this perfect chapel

I see that no color exist in it

There is just a brightness of glory

I began to cry

As I look down at my hand admiring the chapel

Getting a small glimpse of heaven

Sedelia Gardner

The same God

The same God
That gave life to dust
Gave life to me
The same God
That spared Noah
Spared me to
The same God
That guided Moses
Guides me also
The same God
That had confidence in Job
Has confidence in me
The same God
That gave wealth to Joseph
Has given me wealth
The same God
That protected Daniel
Protects me now
The same God
That gave Solomon strength
Gives me strength
The Same God
That spoke to John
Speaks to me
The same God
That died on the cross for you
Died on the cross for me
The same God
That washed away your sins

Ghetto Love: Renaissance

Washed away mines
The same God
The rose from the dead for you
Rose from the dead for me
The same God

Sedelia Gardner

Renaissance

I opened my mouth

And screamed like a newborn baby being born

Feverishly looking around for my mother to nurse me

That is how it felt

When the renaissance hit me

Reborn again

Forgiven of sin

And saved from a life of fire

Was a gift from the renaissance

I opened my eyes

As if I was a newborn baby

Seeing the world for the very first time

The renaissance has now taken away my blindness

Chains broken

Burdens lifted

And a feeling of being free

Was a gift from the renaissance

Sedelia Gardner

Beliefs/Believe

My weight is light

My burdens are few

My belief carries me

I believe in my beliefs

And I trust what I believe

I am guided by my beliefs

My legs tire not

Because my beliefs carries me

My heart is light

My tears are few

My belief carries me

I believe in my beliefs

And I follow what I believe

I am blessed by my beliefs

My body aches not

Because my beliefs carries me

Sedelia Gardner

Fear and Faith

Fear and faith

Cannot dwell in the same heart

A constant feud they will have over you

Until you make your decision

Will you chose faith

And learn to not walk by sight

Or fall captive to fear

And learn to stay still because of what you see

Fear and faith

Cannot dwell in the same heart

There can only be one winner

Which one will you choose

Will you run with faith

Knowing there's an eternal victory up ahead

Or will you run with fear

Down a path of certain damnation

Fear and faith

Ghetto Love: Renaissance

Cannot dwell in the same heart

Never give up on faith

Because faith will never give up on you

But fear fades away once it is beaten

Sedelia Gardner

God grows people

The seed was planted

When the blood was spilled on the ground

Through my down time

My seed still found a way to sprout

On dry ground

During my up times

My leafs began to open

And turn green like the pastures on the other side

And my roots dug deeper into the ground

So when my down time came

I would be untouched by the knife

See God grows people

As I began to grow

From the blood that was shed

My branches started to stretch higher

And even thou the storms came

And some branches were broken

The sun quickly began to shine brighter on me

To heal them

Ghetto Love: Renaissance

See God grows people

I was grown from a drop of blood

And given my form from the word

And even thou I look like a single tree

Standing alone on the open field

I have the unseen surrounding me

See God grows people

Sedelia Gardner

Sedelia Gardner

Potter's Wheel

My beginning started on a potter's wheel

There He slowly tapped the petal

To spin the wheel to give me form

Gently He placed His hands around me

Removing any seen and unseen imperfections

Looking down admiring His work

It was now time to place it in the oven

To bring the impurities from the inside out

So that its usefulness could emerge

His gentle hands remove it from the heat

And He gives a tiny thump on the rim

So that a song can come out

If the melody isn't sweet to His ears

Back to the heat it is returned

To be formed into what it was made for

On the potter's wheel I sit

With His gentle hands surrounding me

Ghetto Love: Renaissance

Softly whispering to my soul

My child whom I love

I must also discipline

Slowly He taps the petal

And gently turns the potter's wheel

Sedelia Gardner

Harvest

This is the year of harvest

My arms are open wide

Ready to receive the wages from my Father

Whom land I have tilled

While He was gone

A strong and faithful servant I have been

And humble during my labors

When the storms came

I did not retreat or seek shelter

When the sun came out to kill the crops

I stood over them and gave them shade

When the rain came down

To wash the crops away

I gathered them up before they were washed away

My Father's garden

I have tended to without complaint

His word said I am blessed

By the works of my hands

Ghetto Love: Renaissance

And my heart has told me that my job is done

This is the year of harvest

My arms are open wide

Ready to receive the wages

From my Father

Sedelia Gardner

Devil's Smile

My legs are tired

I no longer can take another step

The devil smiles

Then a strong gust of wind came along

And pushed me up ahead

I am tired

Of carrying this bag of burdens on my back

They have gotten to heavy

The devil smiles

And suddenly they disappeared

And I continued on walking

I cannot take anymore

All the doors around me are locked

The devil smiles

Then the doors burst open

And I crawled through the rubble

My eyes are weary

I only see the darkness surrounding me

The devil smiles

And suddenly a light began to shine down from heaven

And I followed it

And I continued walking

Sedelia Gardner

Sedelia Gardner

New Owner

I had a fight with the devil today

I told him he had to go

I finally unlocked the doors

To the temple in my chest

And the new owner

Told him to flee

He tried to win me back

By having me hold on to old memories

And replaying old desires in my mind

And making new promises to my heart

But I love my new owner

And my new owner told him

He had to flee

I had a fight with the devil today

And even thou it was hard

I still won

Ghetto Love: Renaissance

He didn't give me a wound

That my new owner could not heal

My new owner loves me

And told him to flee

Sedelia Gardner

Midnight hour

Sitting up at the midnight hour
Replaying the things that
I have done in my past
And I start to remember
The lies
The pain
The anger
The drugs
The alcohol
The abuse
The sex
I broke down and cried during the midnight hour
Trying to comprehend and understand
The forgiveness that God had on me that despite
The lies
The pain
The drugs
The alcohol
The abuse
The sex
He felt it was necessary for Him to come down in
the
Midnight hour off His throne of glory and give His
Life to save mine regardless of the
The lies
The pain
The alcohol

Ghetto Love: Renaissance

The abuse
The sex
I was still worth saving at the midnight hour

Sedelia Gardner

My Gut

Here I am going through this journey

Ignoring the feeling in my gut

The place where my anointing resides

How could I ignore the guidance

Of my own God my creator

How could He be wrong

And I be right

The feeling in my gut

When followed

It has gotten me out of the devils snare

When ignored

He swallowed me whole

But in my gut where my anointing resides

It still gives me guidance in the darkness

Gods anointing did not leave me

Even thou I strayed away

In my heart is where God lives

And His guidance

Comes from my gut

Sedelia Gardner

Holding on

I am not holding on to God

He is holding on to me

It is so easy for me

To turn my back and walk away from Him

And forget about His love

His mercy

His blood

I am not holding on to God

He is holding on to me

It is so easy for me to let Him go and not look back

And forget about His forgiveness

His word

His sacrifice

I am not holding on to God

He is holding on to me

It is hard for Him

To leave me to die

Without putting up a fight for my soul

He said He would never leave me

Never forsake me

But always protect me

I am not holding on to God

He is holding on to me

Sedelia Gardner

Sheppard Call

The Sheppard has come

He is standing on the mountain top

Looking over His land

Calling out to His sheep to come into His pasture

He climbed down off His high mountain top

To open the gate that was closed to some

His faithful sheep heard His call

And they ran to go graze in the green pastures

The Sheppard opens the gate wider

So that the lost sheep may still find a way

To get into His pasture

The Sheppard lets out a call

To those that can hear Him

He leaves His faithful sheep there to graze

Wandering about the land He goes

While graciously gathering His lost sheep

Once they are found by the good Sheppard

Ghetto Love: Renaissance

They run through the gate

That looks narrow to some

To go rest and graze in the green pastures

Sedelia Gardner

Gentle Breeze

Gentle breeze how I embrace you

Your touch is from my savior

Wrap around me gentle breeze

Hold me close to my savior bosom

Gentle breeze how I rejoice

When you touch me

Your touch lets me know

My savior is with me

Let the winds come

From the north, south, east and west

Swirl me up in a rapture of

My savior presence gentle breeze

Sedelia Gardner

Invisible Warrior

Let me kneel down and pray for my invisible
warrior
Who needs some strength
I need his wings to cover me
While I sleep
And I need his wings to cover me
While I walk

Let me kneel down and pray for my invisible
warrior
Who needs some strength
I need his wings to protect me
From the enemy
And I need his wings to protect me
From myself

Let me kneel down and pray for my invisible
warrior
Who needs some strength
I feel the devil trying to creep into me
While I sleep
And I feel him taking over me
While I walk

Let me kneel down and pray for my invisible
warrior
Who needs some strength
I need his wings to surround me
And keep from the enemy

Sedelia Gardner

I need him to fight with me
Against the enemy
Let me kneel down and pray for my invisible
warrior
Who needs some strength

Sedelia Gardner

Broken Vessel

Broken vessel cracked, chipped and dirty

Alone on a shelf no use for anyone around

You are just a place where cob webs hang

And dust can settle for rest

Unable to hold your fill

Of the remembrance wine that seeps through your cracks

Unable to prove your worth

You are placed back on the shelf

And the door closes behind you

Time has passed by

Your lovely paint has now faded

The ones who placed you on the shelf

Have now forgotten you were even there

The hands come down

And gently wrapped around the broken vessel

A gentle breeze came by and blew all the dust

And the cob webs away

Slowly with time the old paint is removed

With His hands He carefully repaints the broken vessel

The chips and cracks were slowly filled

No one can see the broken vessel anymore

But there it sits

The new owner pours the wine

It holds it fill

Nothing else can go through the broken vessel

Sedelia Gardner

Grace

Where are you Grace

Has anyone ever seen your face

Everyone asks for you

But no one has ever seen you

You name is on the lips of the dying

It is screamed out by those that are crying

Where are you Grace

Why haven't I seen your face

Your touch I have felt

It wraps around me like a belt

By you I was saved

And a new road was paved

God has given me a measure of you

Why can't I see you

Everyone asks for you

Will it take a life time to see you

Will see you in the throne room

Or will you find me in my dark gloom

Where are you Grace

Why has no one see your face

But only felt the touch of Grace

Sedelia Gardner

Chase Me

Chase me

Even in the darkness

Where there is no light is up ahead

I want you to keep moving

So run

Chase me

And find what it is

That I have put in you

Others around you have potential

But yours is greater

If you just run

Chase me

And I will reach back behind you

And place you up ahead

And push you

If you just get the courage

To run

Sedelia Gardner

Children do you hear me

Children do you hear me

Has the devil deafen your ears to me

Children do you hear me

Have you forgotten me

I answered your prayers

Children do you hear me

I am here

Stretching my hand out to you

With a bleeding heart

I call to you children

Do you hear me

Has the devil shown you a better way

Children do you hear me

Have you forgotten the cross

That saved you

Children I am here

Screaming out your name

To call you back home

Do you hear me

Sedelia Gardner

Now watch me

Sitting here staring at the black and white

In front of me and getting lost in the conversation

Around me

Slowly forgetting how to handle the situation

Then a voice was carried in on the winds

But I refused to hear it

As I pace the floor

Getting lost in the black and white in front of me

My faith slowly slips away

And my prayers are losing their power

So caught up with what I see

That I forget about the unseen around me

Crying tears for what the black and white is telling me

Not for what the unseen is doing for me

As I stare down at the black and white

It is slowly changing on my behalf

But my faith has slipped away

And I cannot see it

The winds come

And quickly dry up my tears

And the clouds began to form up above me

And a voice rolled off the clouds

Sounding like thunder

And shaking the very ground I stood on

Saying

NOW WATCH ME

Sedelia Gardner

Send me an Angel

Lord please send me an angel

I pray with my mouth

But my faith is weak

And I feel the enemy taking over

I hear him laugh

When I pray to you

I see him smile

When I call out your name

Flee he does not

Instead he takes a seat

I walk

And he is taking over my steps

His grip on me is getting tighter

I am struggling to break away

From him but I can't

I need someone to help me

Fight this take over

I pray with my mouth

But my faith is weak

Lord please send me an angel

Sedelia Gardner

In the deep

I am diving in the waters

And I am going in the deep

I am not looking back

Or coming up for air

Others have already ran to higher grounds

But I keep swimming

In the rough waters

I see the calm up ahead

So I stay in the deep

I am now riding the waves

I am closer to the calm

I am not going back

Even thou others are turning around

I keep on swimming

Catching my breath

As I glide on the waves

Which are no longer against me

I see the calm up ahead

So I stay in the deep

Sedelia Gardner

Sedelia Gardner

Should have been

I was not there in the crowd
To hear Him get His sentence
But I should have been
But He took my place
I was not there to there
To see Him receive His beating
And receive His crown of thorns
I should have been
But He took my place
I was not there
As He carried the cross
On His shoulders to Calvary
I should have been
But He took my place
I was not there
To feel the pain
When the spikes was nailed
Into His hands and feet
And they stretch Him out
And hung Him high
And a spear was driven into His side
As He dropped His head to the side
And He died on the cross
I should have been
But He took my place
I was not there
To witness God raise Him up from the dead
Early Sunday morning

And called Him to take His place
On the right side of the throne
I will be
Because He took my place

Sedelia Gardner

Search Deep

Look at me and tell me what you see

Stare long

And hard

And search deep

Nothing is there you say

Even my enemies search for the scars

They left behind

And they see nothing

The devil came

And he looked at me

He stared long

And hard

And searched deep

Nothing was there for him to find

Who is this person

That does not have a scar from me

No one leave this world untouched

He lashed out at me

But he couldn't leave a scratch

Ghetto Love: Renaissance

He stared long

And hard

And searched deep

God had healed all of my wounds

And the devil couldn't find a single one

God took away the pain

And erased temptation from my mind

And filled me with His spirit

Look at me and tell me what you see

Stare long

And hard

And search deep

Sedelia Gardner

Spirit Man

Spirit Man

Please go to the throne room

A place where my flesh cannot enter

And make a plea on my behalf

You were sealed up

But now I have unleashed you

Spirit man

I prayed to keep you safe from harm

I used my faith to give you strength

I have unleashed you

You are now free

Spirit man

Use my faith

To go and unlock the great doors to the throne room

Pled to the Father

On my behalf

Tell Him I am one of His humble faithful servants

Ask Him to remember me

His child whom He loves

Beg Him to give me rest

Spirit man

Sedelia Gardner

Heavenly Grass

I stand humbly beneath your feet

Looking up at the skies

Admiring the grasses of heaven

As they float by

How carefully they float

Never falling down

Never forgetting their purpose

I watch as they change shape

Being reformed and being reborn

Turning into something

So wonderful I can't explain

And I don't have the power to question You

All I can do is watch and trust You

Knowing that this change will bring me rest

I watch the grasses of heaven

As they float by

Coming together to give shade when needed

Breaking apart giving light to things that need growth

How carefully they float

Never falling down

Never forgetting their purpose

Sedelia Gardner

Sedelia Gardner

Anointing

Anointing stick to me

Like a spider does to her web

Protect me and seal me up

As if I were a precious pearl inside an oyster shell

Soar high above the clouds

Stretch out your eagle wings

And I will lay protected underneath their shadow

Stand your ground

Like a raging bull

When the enemy comes for me

Let out a loud lions roar

So that the devil knows who his king is

Place sweetness on my lips

Like that of honey from a honey comb

So when I speak

They only hear the anointing

Sedelia Gardner

Broken

The devil tried to cloud my eyes
Burden my heart
And make me stumble as I walked
But God cleared my vision
Lightened my load
And picked me up after every fall
Broken were the chains

Broken when I called out your name
Broken when I knelt down and prayed
Broken when I read the word
Broken when I repented
Broken when I realized who died and rose for me

The devil tried to hold my head down
Kill my spirit
And take my happiness away as I rejoiced
But God lifted up my head through the pain
Touched my spirit
And put joy deep down in my soul
Broken were the chains

Sedelia Gardner

Survivor

Pretty white wings hang on the ground

Collecting the dirt left behind after the battle

Lord if you love me let me die

Was the only thing I could think of

I lost touch of the battle I had won

My mind was only concentrating on the pain

That I didn't even notice that the battle

Had now turned into dust beneath my feet

A victory uncelebrated

Mourning in the dirt with a hanging head

When my wings should have been raised up

And spread wide open

So that the dirt could fall off

But instead they hung low

Thinking about the pain of the past

Lord if you love me let me die

I thought again to myself

A swirling wind came

And the dirt from the battle dropped from my wings

Ghetto Love: Renaissance

I was unable to hold on to the dirt

And it now lay beneath my feet

Where it was placed by the winds

I began to open my wings

And spread them wide in the glory of God

The swirling winds lifted me high

Above the battlefield

And I was able to see all that I have slaughtered

Not a single one was standing

All were dead beneath my feet like dirt

There I stood in victory

The survivor

Sedelia Gardner

Balance

Cup your hands together

Dip them in the water

Lift them up high

So not a single drop slips out

Now walk forward

Balance yourself

So that you do not sway from left to right

Showing one side more favor than the other

But walk on a straight path

Always moving forward

Not losing a single drop along the way

You can't do it you say

But yet we are like drops of water

And God holds us all in His hands

He is forever moving forward

Never losing a single drop

Never showing one man more favor than the next

But giving favor based on their faith in Him

Ghetto Love: Renaissance

A type of travel you endure

Being cupped in His hands

Always moving forward

And never slipping out

And never left behind

Sedelia Gardner

Protection

The storms have come

And taken my shelter from over my head

My family has ran away

Because of their fear of tomorrow

Even the threads of my clothing

Has lost their grip and turned to rags

As I wear them on my back

All of the protection that I had

Made with my hands is now gone

And is just a memory in my mind

And now I lay here uncovered

In the eyes of my enemies

But I was born with protection instilled in me

A gift from the cross

I had to lose the protection made by my hands

In order to open the gift inside

To receive the protection made by His hands

A protection that will never leave me

Ghetto Love: Renaissance

Or wither away in the wind

But will always be with me

During all the storms I face

Sedelia Gardner

Mountain top

I am going to a place where the air is thin

And the climate is cold

I received a glimpse of who I am

And what I am

And He then locked the door

And said follow me

And placed the key in His pocket and proceeded to walk up the mountain

The air is thin but I followed behind Him

The climate changed along the way

But it was not the glimpse I received

So I did not stop

I kept on chasing Him up to the place where the air is thin

I wanted to turn around

But I wanted the key

I wanted to stop

But I wanted the key

The air is thin but I kept on chasing Him

Until we reached the top

And I can see the person who was on the bottom

And that person is not the same person who now stands on

The mountain top

Where the air is thin

And the climate is cold

Sedelia Gardner

Cloud without rain

I was a cloud without rain

Unable to give life to my own seed

That I had planted

No harvest did I receive from the dry ground

Beneath my feet

The rocks began to cry out

And the dirt begged for rain to come

But I was just a cloud without rain

Unable to satisfy the thirst of my own crops

So that I may reap a harvest for my labor

I stood on barren land

I toiled the land but it remained dry

With nothing left but a tear left in my soul

I released that tear drop

And it was caught before it hit the ground

And placed back into my cloud

He held the rain in

The season had not come for my barren land to receive its rain

Ghetto Love: Renaissance

A cloud without rain

I was floating over a desolate land

My soul screamed out in surrenderence to Him

And the rain that He held in was now released

And life was given to my land

Sedelia Gardner

Pain/Faith

Pain *you were a place made for me to visit*
Only for a little while not stay there and hold
On to you after the issue has been solved by **Faith**

Faith *come and pry lose my fingers from the door*
Frame of pain the issue has been solved but fear of
What is next keeps me holding on to **Pain**

Pain *my ignorance keeps me holding on to you*
Even though the blood washed you away my eyes
Are too blind to see that I can be healed through my **Faith**

Faith *where are you come and push me into your belly*
So that I can nestle there as if I were in my mother's womb
Safe and untouched by **Pain**

Pain *if I let you go I can receive the promises written*
Down for me in the Word based on my **Faith**

Faith *you hold hands with pain you are my weapon*
Against it all I must use you so that no victories are awarded
To **Pain**

Sedelia Gardner

The Pit

Lord, pull me out of this abyss of darkness
I have placed myself in
Let the prayers that I have in the storehouse
Fall down on me
Let the words of the prayers that have been
Said on my behalf hook my soul and
Pull me out of this pit

Lord, pull me out of this darkness
That surrounds me
Let your word seep into me
And hook my soul
To open up my chest and release me
From this darkness I have put myself in
Grab hold of me Lord and
Pull me out of this pit

Lord, pull me out this darkness
Let the hymns of the church
Reach my ears and hook my soul
Let someone come to me
So we can touch and agree for my release
So I can be lifted out of this pit

Lord, pull me out of this abyss of darkness
Where my soul has fell asleep in
Let my tears fall down and wash me
Let your love hook into my soul

To save me and
Pull me out of this pit

Sedelia Gardner

The seed

I am grinded down to the core

This empty shell has been broken

The only thing left is this un-sprouted seed

The seed that was placed in me when you died

But it never took root

Lord, take this seed it is all that is left

And place it in your garden

Give this seed a second chance to sprout

Into the tree you made it to be

Let my roots grow and run deep into the ground

Never to be severed again

Let me sprout through the dirt that was thrown on me

Let my body rise up and continue to forever

Reach towards the light above

Let branches form on me so I can reach out to you

In every situation

Let my testimonies float in the winds

Like leaves only to fall on the ones who need strength

Lord, take this seed it is all that is left

And place it in your garden

Sedelia Gardner

Rain

We forgot about the rain

And the land dried up

Let your word rain down

And pour life into this dry land

Let your children remember that they need your rain

For the crops that they now have are temporary

The rain they have won't give life to the land

After the harvest

Let your word rain down

And pour life into this dry land

Let your children remember the rains of their ancestors

Let it flow like a mighty river

Going into the deepest places inside of us

Leaving nothing untouched

Wash us dear Lord

To remind us that we need your rain

To harvest a everlasting crop

Sedelia Gardner

Blessing in the room

There is a blessing in this room today
And my soul knows that I need it
But my flesh is telling me everything is alright
But I am surrounded by people
Who are pulling it down so I can receive it
They know I need the blessing
I listen to the groans they are letting out for me
So my soul can receive what it needs
The sounds of their groans etch out the doubt in
my soul

There is a blessing in this room today
And my soul knows that I need it
But my flesh is telling me to turn and walk away
But I am surrounded by people
Who are pulling it down so I can receive it
I listen to the songs they are singing for me
So my soul can receive what it needs
The sounds of their voices erase the doubt in mind

There is a blessing in this room today
And my soul knows that I need it
But my flesh is telling me to give up
But I am surrounded by people
Who know I need the blessing
I listen to the scriptures they are saying for me
So my soul can receive what it needs
The sounds of the Lord Words wash away all doubt
in my heart

Ghetto Love: Renaissance

There is a blessing in this room today
And my soul is ready to receive it
My flesh can no longer turn me from it
I am surrounded by people
Who pulled it down for me
The groans
The songs
And the scriptures
Have made me strong enough to open up my arms
And cast all doubt aside
So I can retrieve it

Sedelia Gardner

Battle Scars

I stand in the mirror

And I look at my unseen and seen battle scars

To remind me of how bad the enemy wanted me dead

My battles scars

The seen battle scars are for you to see

They are nothing more but endless victories against the enemy

When you have doubt

Lord said look at me

When you have worries

Lord said look at me

When you have fear

Lord said look at me

When you need strength

Lord said look at me

When you need healing

Lord said look at me

When you need faith

Lord said look at me

Ghetto Love: Renaissance

The unseen battle scars are for me to see

Those are unseen battle won with victories against the enemy

When I have doubt

Lord said look at yourself

When I have worries

Lord said look at yourself

When I have fear

Lord said look at yourself

When I need strength

Lord said look at yourself

When I need healing

Lord said look at yourself

When I need faith

Lord said look at yourself

I stand in the mirror

And I look at my unseen and seen battle scars

To remind myself of how bad my God wanted me to live

Sedelia Gardner

The Bank

I finally made my trip
To the Bank early this Sunday morning
So I could open my new account
Since I had left everything behind
The only thing I had to deposit
Was a thread of hope that lined my pocket
I approached the teller
And He quickly told me
That no application was needed
His bank rejects no one
But all that I had to do was
Empty out what I had and give it all to Him
And He will take care of the rest He said
I reached down in my pockets
And give Him my short thread of hope
Check again He said
Make sure all your pockets are empty
I want everything He said with a smile
I don't want you to be weighed down He said
And Shockley I had some lose change
In one of my back pockets
Things I had forgot I was still even carrying
around
I looked at the teller
And asked are you sure you want me to deposit
These items
Yes He replied my Bank is strong enough
To hold anything
Here is my pain
Disappointments

Anguish and fears
Neglects
Stress and worries
Here is my Confusion
Distress and depression
Despair
Anxiety and Anger
Abuse and addiction
And a mountain of tears
Thank you He replied as He smiled and took it all
And He placed my deposit into His vault
Now go enjoy your new bank account
He replied as He returned my thread of hope
It had gotten a little longer since I had
Placed it in His hands

Sedelia Gardner

5

Sedelia Gardner

Prayer

Prayer is an unseen force
My God is an unseen force
Prayer can make a mountain move
My God can make a mountain move
All powerful is prayer
All powerful is my God
Why should I not pray when the force of my prayer
Is just as powerful as the God I serve
Why should I not pray when my prayers can move
mountains
Just like the God I serve
Prayers get answers
My God give answers
Prayers are real
My God is real
Why should I not pray when my prayers get
answered
From the God I serve
Why should I not pray when my prayers are just as
real
As the God I serve
Prayer works
My God works
Prayer changes things
My God make things change
Why should I not pray when my prayers work on
my behalf?
Just like the God I serve
Why should I not pray when my prayers changes
things for me

Ghetto Love: Renaissance

Just like the God I serve
I pray
Jesus prayed
The Angels pray
Satan prayed
This powerful unseen force
That can get answers and turn things around
Is a simple Prayer

Sedelia Gardner

Master

Yes I am a slave

I was born a slave

But deciding on which master to serve

Was a choice put into my hands

Shall I serve the master that beats me?

With the whip until I bleed

Or shall I serve the master that shields me

From the whip so that my blood is not shed

Two masters

One slave

Were shall I go

The choice is in my hands

Shall I serve the master that drains me?

Until there is no life left in me

Or shall I serve the master that

Has promised everlasting life to me

One soul

Two forces

What should I do?

That choice is in my hands

Shall I serve the master whose foot is kept on the back of his servants?

And their faces forever laying in the dirt

Or shall I serve the master that

Who helps his servants to stand up at all times?

And make sure their eyes are forever looking up

One body

Two houses

Where will my house be?

The choice lays in my hands

Sedelia Gardner

Stuck in the middle

Two against one

I am stuck in the middle

Each promising me some type of reward

Each blessing me with something to survive on

One has power

And one has to ask for power in order to move

The decision has caused my flesh to tear from my bones

And fall to the ground

Those on the side of me fight to gather my pieces

Each with a promise to make me whole

Two against one

I am stuck in the middle

Each promising to meet my needs

Each showing me that they can

One has power

And one has to gather others in order to get power

The decision has caused my soul to shatter into pieces

Those on the side of me send out their armies to fight and gather my pieces

Each with a promise of giving me a room in their house

Two against one

I am stuck in the middle

Who will gather the most pieces?

Who will I let keep the pieces they have gathered

To make me whole

Sedelia Gardner

Many Tears

Many tears
Many tears
Many tears I have cried
I have cried many tears
But I have turned them over to God
In return He has used the tears
To sprout strength in me
Many tears
Many tears
Many tears I have cried
I have cried many tears
But only some could be seen by God
In return He used my tears
To fertile the ground beneath me
Many tears
Many tears
Many tears I have cried

I have cried many tears
But the number is only known to God
In return He used the tears
To pour blessing upon me
Many tears
Many tears
Many tears I have cried
I have cried many tears
But I still pray to my God
In return He gathers up my tears
To rewrite them into a testimony for me
Many tears
Many tears
Many tears I have cried

Sedelia Gardner

Unknown tongue

The Holy Spirit took me into the presence of the Lord

And I opened my mouth to speak

But the word of man was released

And God heard me not

Holy Spirit why bring me to my Lord

And His ears hear me not

And I opened my mouth to speak

But the word of man was now bound

And God heard me

With every groan that I released into the air

One of my enemies fell at my feet

And as I began to speak

My unknown tongue was released into the air

My harvest basket began to fill itself

And my unknown tongue had retrieved all that was taken from me

My prayers have now turned from flesh to spirit

And they can now reach my God ears

My unknown tongue can release angels into battle

With every step that I take I am surrounded by warriors

The Holy Spirit took me into the presence of God

So that I could be added to the Lords army

Unknown tongue remember me

When you go talk to my God

He cannot hear the cries of my flesh

So ask Him for mercy

Beg for His favor

And plead for His love

Sedelia Gardner

Victory

Enemy don't laugh at me

Because you see tears

Falling from my eyes

Don't rejoice just yet

Why crowd around me and dance

Because I am on my knees

Have you already won the victory over me?

My enemies have you forgotten about the WORD

"Victory" is mine said the Lord

Enemy don't laugh at me

Because you see tears

Falling from my eyes

Don't rejoice just yet

Because they are tears of Victory

Not tears of defeat

You can crowd around me and dance

Because I am on my knees

Giving thanks

Not because I am broken

Have you really won the victory over me?

Even in my torn and battered state

"Victory" is mine said the Lord

Sedelia Gardner

Lose Ground

I will not lose ground

I fought too hard on the battlefield to gain it

My ancestors prayed for me to have it

And I will not give it up

Fight with me if you dare

The blood of my ancestors travels through me

Their prayers are breaking down the doors of the store house

Ready to engage in battle

I will not lose ground

I fought too hard on the battlefield to gain it

My tears have fertilized the ground

My harvest is near

I will not give it up

Fight with me if you dare

Even my ancestors that dwell with you in hell

Cry for me to stand against you

Their screams strengthens my soul

I will not lose ground

Fight with me if you dare

Come out of the shadows

And unto the battlefield

And let the strength of my prayers cut you into pieces

Not a stone will you take from my lot

I will not lose ground

Sedelia Gardner

Bow Down

His mercy is immeasurable

That the great kings of the land bow down

The reach of His hand is unreachable by His creations

That even the elders bow down

His favor unseen is begged for by the greatest warriors

That even they bow down

The love He has no limit

That even those that are lost when found will bow down

His grace is given to those that believe in Him

That those that receive it bow down

His power that has no end that even in His presence

Demons must bow down

The angels who have more power than me

Grace His ears with endless songs of praise

His glory to great to look upon makes them bow down

Who am I?

103

That I cannot drop my head and bend my knees

My mercy can be measured

My hand can be reached

My favor can be seen

My love is limited

I have no grace to give

And power I have not without Him

So I must bow down

Sedelia Gardner

First Offering

My eyes close to the light of the moon
And began to open as the rays of the sun
Dance upon my eye lids
Before I begin to fully awake from my night
slumber
And begin to think thoughts of the day
My first offering of praise should be to Him
It was His grace that covered me
Like a blanket as I slept
Under the light of the moon
And the curtain of stars
And it was His mercy that allowed the rays of the
sun
To rise me from my peaceful slumber
And take a breath
My first offering of praise should be to Him
I sleep peacefully next to my spouse
Under the light of the moon in their arms
But their presence does not guarantee
That I will rise with morning sun
My first offering of praise should be to Him
My provider
My comforter
My healer
My protector
My Father
My every thing
My first offering of praise should be to Him

Sedelia Gardner

Tarry

There is a tarry in my spirit
And it is down deep
I find myself repeating the same prayer
Over and over
My eyes are open
Because Lord you have opened them
So I know I can see
But what is it that is unseen that is causing
This tarry to sit upon me
I speak in an unknown tongue
And moan in pains of labor
Trying to release this tarry
From my spirit
Take it away from me Lord I cry out
As my tears flow from my eyes
Trying to wash the tarry from my spirit
Is there a word I do not know my Lord
That needs to be said
I thought they were all etched in my soul
Scripture after scripture
Roll off of my tongue
But the tarry moves not
Who's burden do I carry Lord
Or is there a blessing that I need to deliverer for
You
So this tarry can unload from my spirit
And let go of my spirit
I pray with more than one
So I know not who this tarry belongs to
Open your mouth

And cry out to the Lord I tell them all
Sing songs of praise and worship to the Lord
Thank Him for His mercy and love
Open up to Him
So this Tarry can be purged from deep inside my
soul

Sedelia Gardner

Take it back

Give that back to me
I command the devil
As he snatched away my dreams
And aspirations that had been with me
Since I was born into this world
They were unused he replied
Even the blessing that were attached to them
Because I did not have enough faith
To make them manifest there are his to take
So I did not fight
His words were true
And the emptiness was felt in my soul
He returned to pull from me
Friendships and relationships
He even had the strength to break the bond between
Mother and child
Husband and wife
And he began to swallow my children into the dark abyss
I screamed for him to give them back
As I tried to hold on to them
He said these are people you did not value
Why keep worthless items around
So I did not fight
His words were true
And the emptiness was felt in my soul
I had opened up the door for chaos to enter into my life
I let him in willingly
And everything was taken from me

Even the clothes from back were cast into darkness
So deep that my hands were unable to reach them
So there I sat
I was left naked in the dirt
Left with only tears
And the word that was etched in my soul
That he could not reach to take away
In my Father arms is where I laid and rested
My tears dropped into the palm of His hands
And my Father took each tear
And turned it into armor and placed the pieces on
my back
He took the word that was etched in my soul
And formed it into a mighty sword
Give everything you have taken from me back
I commanded the devil
As I walked into the pits of hell
Crumbling walls with my words
And making the foundation shake as I stood my
ground
Cutting the chains around me with my sword
One by one
My items were returned to me
And the emptiness began to disappear
I have my armor
My sword
My faith
And now I sit untouched in the palm of my Fathers
hand

Sedelia Gardner

Willow

I fell in love with a weeping willow tree

As I stood alone in a field of darkness

Underneath her hanging branches for safety

Low they hung

But weak they are not

God gentle breeze glides through her hanging limbs

Gently touching me

Slowly raising my head

And softly catching tears

Her branches sway in the winds

Looking like puppet strings

Being controlled by our unseen creator

Low she hangs

But weak she is not

Her hanging branches gently lift me up

In the middle of this dark field

I fell in love with a weeping willow tree

As her branches hung low

Grabbing me and twirling me around

Ghetto Love: Renaissance

On her puppet strings

In the darkness

Controlled by our creator

Sedelia Gardner

Remnant

I was made to be woven into a quilt

A pattern designed before I came into existence

A mere remnant

I resemble through the eyes of many

But yet I am part of the quilt

Remnants of fabrics tossed aside

Un-useful by many

Because of their unraveling

And their inability to look like those pieces that surrounds it

But yet they were created

For a purpose

The quilt was woven

And the designed was chosen before I came into existence

And even thou many look at me

As a mere remnant on the floor

My Father felt I was a much needed piece

And I had a specific place on His quilt

A place chosen before I took my first breath

Ghetto Love: Renaissance

Sewn into His quilt with the word I was

With thread covered with His blood

To keep it in place

Never to fall lose

But to remain whole to the quilt

Never again to be a mere remnant laying upon the dust on the floor

But to put glee into the eyes of those that look upon it

The unraveling cease to exist

Even the eyes of the ones who saw it

Seen it no more

The unwanted piece no longer looked like a useless remnant

As it was stitched into place

And was woven into the Fathers quilt

Sedelia Gardner

Field of weeds

Seeded from a beautiful flower

I was

And then planted in a field of weeds

Which out numbered me

The bright sun shone brightly upon them

And the rain hit them first

Only leaving behind small drops

For me to gather

But there I was

Growing silently beneath them

When I should have died

But season

After season

After season

I grew

Even if I was too small to be noticed by some

I still lived

The weeds gathered all the rays from the sun

But yet they died

They soaked up more rain than their roots could handle

But yet they died

They stood over me looking down at me

But yet they died

Their shadows blocked me out

But yet they died

Some were even pulled up by their roots

When it was time for the farmer to prepare for the harvest

But season

After season

After season

I grew

And I was soon growing in a field of flowers

The weeds had all disappeared

Away from the field they once overran

And now the sun shines brightly upon me

And my branches stretch out wide

To embrace the falling rain that was once stolen from me

I am now reaching places I could not reach before

My roots dig down deep beneath me

Grabbing hold of the foundation

That held me up in the field of weeds

Sedelia Gardner

Caterpillar

There you are caterpillar

How unattractive you look to my eyes

The colors that cover you

Are unpleasing to me

The way you chose to move along your path

Disgust me

But there you are caterpillar

Gods will made a way for you

To crawl through destruction

Even I cannot destroy you

As you crawl beneath my feet

Crawl caterpillar

Gather what you need along the way

To help you make it to your destination

My eyes cannot yet see what is inside

Gods will has encased you inside a cocoon

For you to wait there

Until the caterpillar has completely disappeared

New colors emerge from the cocoon

That God had encased you in

That pleases all that see them

Spread your wings butterfly

And glide through the winds

I am struck down by envy

While admiring your beauty

Not even remembering that you were once a

Caterpillar

Sedelia Gardner

Ghetto Love: Renaissance

Dear God,

I made my bed on a pile of rocks

I caused my own storms

I turned away from You and caused my own pain

I allowed destruction to come into my life

I gave up on myself and You

I lost my faith

I forgot about the cross

But You chased after me still

You pulled me out of an endless abyss

And unwrapped me from a vortex of chaos

Where would I be without You?

Sincerely the Child you found!

Sedelia Gardner

NAMES FOR GOD

- **ELOHIM......Genesis 1:1, Psalm 19:1**

- meaning "God", a reference to God's power and might.

- **ADONAI......Malachi 1:6**

- meaning "Lord", a reference to the Lordship of God.

- **JEHOVAH--YAHWEH.....Genesis 2:4**

- a reference to God's divine salvation.

- **JEHOVAH-MACCADDESHEM .Exodus 31:13**

- meaning "The Lord thy sanctifier"

- **JEHOVAH-ROHI......Psalm 23:1**

- meaning "The Lord my shepherd"

- **JEHOVAH-SHAMMAH.......Ezekiel 48:35**

- meaning "The Lord who is present"

- **JEHOVAH-RAPHA.........Exodus 15:26**

- meaning "The Lord our healer"

- **JEHOVAH-TSIDKENU......Jeremiah 23:6**

- meaning "The Lord our righteousness"

- **JEHOVAH-JIREH.........Genesis 22:13-14**

- meaning "The Lord will provide"

- **JEHOVAH-NISSI.........Exodus 17:15**

- meaning "The Lord our banner"

- JEHOVAH-SHALOM........Judges 6:24

- meaning "The Lord is peace"

- JEHOVAH-SABBAOTH......Isaiah 6:1-3

- meaning "The Lord of Hosts"

- JEHOVAH-GMOLAH........Jeremiah 51:6

- meaning "The God of Recompense"

- EL-ELYON....Genesis 14:17-20,Isaiah 14:13-14

- meaning "The most high God"

- EL-ROI................Genesis 16:13

- meaning "The strong one who sees"

- EL-SHADDAI............Genesis 17:1,Psalm 91:1

- meaning "The God of the mountains or God Almighty"

- EL-OLAM...............Isaiah 40:28-31

- meaning "The everlasting God"

MORE NAMES FOR GOD

- AVENGER..........................1Thess.4:6

- ABBA..............................Romans 8:15

- ADVOCATE..........................I John 2:1 (kjv)

- ALMIGHTY..........................Genesis 17:1

- ALL IN ALL.......................Colossians 3:11

- ALPHA..............................Revelation 22:13

- AMEN..............................Revelation 3:14

- ANCIENT OF DAYS..................Daniel 7:9

- ANOINTED ONE....................Psalm 2:2

- APOSTLE..........................Hebrews 3:1

- ARM OF THE LORD..................Isaiah 53:1

- AUTHOR OF ETERNAL SALVATION......
  Hebrews 5:9

- AUTHOR OF OUR FAITH.........Hebrews 12:2

- AUTHOR OF PEACE..................1 Cor. 14:33

- BEGINNING.......................Revelation 21:6

- BISHOP OF SOULS..................1 Peter 2:25

- BLESSED & HOLY RULER...........1 Timothy
  6:15

- BRANCH...........................Jeremiah 33:15

- BREAD OF GOD.....................John 6:33

- BREAD OF LIFE....................John 6:35

- BREATH OF LIFE...Genesis 2:7, Revelation
  11:11

- BRIDEGROOM.......................Isaiah 62:5

- BRIGHT MORNING STAR...Revelation 22:16

- BUCKLER........2 Sam.22:31kjv,Psalm
  18:2kjv,Psalm 18:30kjv,Proverbs 2:7kjv

122

- CAPTAIN OF SALVATION.......Hebrews 2:10

- CARPENTER..........................Mark 6:3

- CHIEF SHEPHERD....................1 Peter 5:4

- CHOSEN ONE.........................Isaiah 42:1

- CHRIST.............................Matthew 22:42

- CHRIST OF GOD......................Luke 9:20

- CHRIST THE LORD....................Luke 2:11

- CHRIST, SON OF LIVING GOD.....Matthew 16:16

- COMFORTER..........................John 14:26(kjv)

- COMMANDER..........................Isaiah 55:4

- CONSOLATION OF ISRAEL.........Luke 2:25

- CONSUMING FIRE....................Deut. 4:24, Heb. 12:29

- CORNERSTONE........................Isaiah 28:16

- COUNSELOR..........................Isaiah 9:6

- CREATOR............................1 Peter 4:19

- CROWN OF BEAUTY....................Isaiah 28:5

- DAYSPRING..........................Luke 1:78

- DELIVERER..........................Romans 11:26

- DESIRED OF ALL NATIONS.........Haggai 2:7

- DIADEM OF BEAUTY...................Isaiah 28:5

- DOOR....................................John 10:7(kjv)

- DWELLING LACE..........................Psalm 90:1

- ELECT ONE..............................Isaiah 42:1

- EMMANUEL..............................Matthew 1:23(kjv)

- END....................................Revelation 21:6

- ETERNAL GOD...........................Deut. 33:27

- ETERNAL LIFE...........................1 John 5:20

- ETERNAL SPIRIT........................Hebrews 9:14

- EVERLASTING FATHER............Isaiah 9:6

- EVERLASTING GOD.........................Genesis 21:33

- EXCELLENT...................Psalm 148:13(kjv)

- FAITHFUL & TRUE........................Revelation 19:11

- FAITHFUL WITNESS.......................Revelation 1:5

- FATHER..................................Matthew 6:9

- FIRSTBORN.......Rom.8:29,Rev.1:5,Col.1:15

- FIRSTFRUITS............................1 Cor.15:20-23

- FORTRESS...............................Jeremiah 16:19

- FOUNDATION............................1 Cor. 3:11

- FOUNTAIN OF LIVING WATERS..............Jeremiah 2:13

- FRIEND..................................Matthew 11:19

- FULLERS'SOAP.................Malachi 3:2(kjv)

- GENTLE WHISPER.................1 Kings 19:12

- GIFT OF GOD...........................John 4:10

- GLORY OF THE LORD....................Isaiah 40:5

- GOD...................................Genesis 1:1

- GOD ALMIGHTY...........................Genesis 17:1

- GOD OF THE WHOLE EARTH....Isaiah 54:5

- GOD OVER ALL...........................Romans 9:5

- GOD WHO SEES ME................Genesis 16:13

- GOODNESS.............................Psalm 144:2(kjv)

- GOOD SHEPHERD.........................John 10:11

- GOVERNOR..............................Psalm 22:28(kjv)

- GREAT HIGH PRIEST...............Hebrews 4:14

- GREAT SHEPHERD...................Hebrews 13:20

- GUIDE..................................Psalm 48:14

- HEAD OF THE BODY.............Colossians 1:18

- HEAD OF THE CHURCH.......Ephesians 5:23

- HEIR OF ALL THINGS...............Hebrews 1:2

- HIDING PLACE...........................Psalm 32:7

- HIGHEST...............................Luke 1:76

125

- HIGH PRIEST..............................Hebrews 3:1
- HIGH PRIEST FOREVER..........Hebrews 6:20
- HOLY GHOST............................John 14:26
- HOLY ONE..............................Acts 2:27
- HOLY ONE OF ISRAEL...................Isaiah 49:7
- HOLY SPIRIT............................John 15:26
- HOPE...................................Titus 2:13
- HORN OF SALVATION.....................Luke 1:69
- HUSBAND....Isaiah 54:5,Jere.31:32,Hosea 2:16
- I AM...............................Exodus 3:14, John 8:58
- IMAGE OF GOD............................2 Cor. 4:4
- IMAGE OF HIS PERSON.....Hebrews 1:3 (kjv)
- IMMANUEL...............................Isaiah 7:14
- INTERCESSOR.....Romans 8:26,27,34 Hebrews 7:25
- JAH..................................Psalm 68:4(kjv)
- JEALOUS............................Exodus 34:14(kjv)
- JEHOVAH.............................Psalm 83:18(kjv)
- JESUS................................Matthew 1:21
- JESUS CHRIST OUR LORD.......Romans 6:23
- JUDGE.......................Isaiah 33:22, Acts 10:42
- JUST ONE.............................Acts 22:14

126

- KEEPER.............................Psalm 121:5

- KING...............................Zechariah 9:9

- KING ETERNAL.........................1 Timothy 1:17

- KING OF GLORY.........................Psalm 24:10

- KING OF JEWS..........................Matthew 27:11

- KING OF KINGS.........................1 Timothy 6:15

- KING OF SAINTS.......................Revelation 15:3

- LAMB OF GOD...........................John 1:29

- LAST ADAM.............................1 Cor. 15:45

- LAWGIVER..............................Isaiah 33:22

- LEADER................................Isaiah 55:4

- LIFE...................................John 14:6

- LIGHT OF THE WORLD...................John 8:12

- LIKE AN EAGLE.........................Deut. 32:11

- LILY OF THE VALLEYS..................Song 2:1

- LION OF THE TRIBE OF JUDAH...Revelation 5:5

- LIVING GOD............................Daniel 6:20

- LIVING STONE.........................1 Peter 2:4

- LIVING WATER.........................John 4:10

- LORD.................................John 13:13

- LORD GOD ALMIGHTY......Revelation 15:3

- **LORD JESUS CHRIST**....................1 Cor. 15:57
- **LORD OF ALL**............................Acts 10:36
- **LORD OF GLORY** ....1 Cor. 2:8
- **LORD OF HARVEST**..............Matthew 9:38
- **LORD OF HOSTS**........................Haggai 1:5
- **LORD OF LORDS**........................1 Tim. 6:15
- **LORD OUR RIGHTEOUSNESS**..Jeremiah 23:6
- **LOVE**................................1 John 4:8
- **LOVINGKINDNESS**......................Psalm 144:2
- **MAKER**............................Job 35:10, Psalm 95:6
- **MAJESTY ON HIGH**.......................Hebrews 1:3
- **MAN OF SORROWS**........................Isaiah 53:3
- **MASTER**................................Luke 5:5
- **MEDIATOR**...............................1 Timothy 2:5
- **MERCIFUL GOD**.....................Jeremiah 3:12
- **MESSENGER OF THE COVENANT**....Malachi 3:1
- **MESSIAH**................................ John 4:25
- **MIGHTY GOD**...............................Isaiah 9:6
- **MIGHTY ONE**...............................Isaiah 60:16
- **MOST UPRIGHT**............................Isaiah 26:7
- **NAZARENE**.................................Matthew 2:23

- **OFFSPRING OF DAVID**.......Revelation 22:16

- **OMEGA**.....................................Revelation 22:13

- **ONLY BEGOTTEN SON**.........John 1:18(kjv)

- **OUR PASSOVER LAMB**.................1 Cor. 5:7

- **OUR PEACE**...............................Ephesians 2:14

- **PHYSICIAN**...............................Luke 4:23

- **PORTION**...............Psalm 73:26,Psalm 119:57

- **POTENTATE**...............................1 Timothy 6:15

- **POTTER**...................................Isaiah 64:8

- **POWER OF GOD**............................1 Cor. 1:24

- **PRINCE OF LIFE**...........................Acts 3:15

- **PRINCE OF PEACE**.........................Isaiah 9:6

- **PROPHET**.................................Acts 3:22

- **PROPHET OF THE HIGHEST**........Luke 1:76

- **PROPITIATION**..........1John 2:2, 1John 4:10

- **PURIFIER**.................................Malachi 3:3

- **QUICKENING SPIRIT**........1 Corinthians 15:45(kjv)

- **RABBONI (TEACHER)**.............John 20:16

- **RADIANCE OF GOD'S GLORY**....Heb.1:3

- **REDEEMER**...............................Job 19:25

- **REFINER'S FIRE**..........................Malachi 3:2

- REFUGE.................................Jeremiah 16:19

- RESURRECTION............................John 11:25

- REWARDER...............................Hebrews 11:6

- RIGHTEOUS ONE...........................1 John 2:1

- ROCK....................................1 Cor.10:4

- ROOT OF DAVID............................Rev. 22:16

- ROSE OF SHARON..........................Song 2:1

- RULER OF GOD'S CREATION........Rev. 3:14

- RULER OVER KINGS OF EARTH....Rev 1:5

- RULER OVER ISRAEL..............Micah 5:2

- SAVIOR...................................Luke 2:11

- SCEPTRE.................................Numbers 24:17

- SEED....................................Genesis 3:15

- SERVANT.................................Isaiah 42:1

- SHADE...................................Psalm 121:5

- SHEPHERD OF OUR SOULS......1Peter 2:25

- SHIELD..................................Genesis 15:1

- SHILOH..................................Genesis 49:10

- SONG..........................Exodus 15:2, Isaiah 12:2

- SON OF DAVID............................Matthew 1:1

- SON OF GOD..............................Matthew 27:54

- SON OF MAN...............................Matthew 8:20

- SON OF THE MOST HIGH............Luke 1:32

- SOURCE....................................Hebrews 5:9

- SPIRIT.....................................John 4:24

- SPIRIT OF ADOPTION............Romans 8:15

- SPIRIT OF GOD............................Genesis 1:2

- SPIRIT OF TRUTH....John 14:17,15:26,16:13

- STAR OUT OF JACOB.........Numbers 24:17

- STRENGTH...............................Jeremiah 16:19

- STONE.....................................1 Peter 2:8

- STONE OF ISRAEL...............Genesis 49:24

- STRONGHOLD.............................Nahum 1:7

- STRONG TOWER.................Proverbs 18:10

- SUN OF RIGHTEOUSNESS.......Malachi 4:2

- TEACHER...................................John 13:13

- TEMPLE....................................Revelation 21:22

- THE ONE....................................Psalm 144:2,10

- TRUE LIGHT...............................John 1:9

- TRUE WITNESS....................Revelation 3:14

- TRUTH......................................John 14:6

- VINE...John 15:5

- WALL OF FIRE...............................Zechariah 2:5

- WAY..John 14:6

- WISDOM OF GOD..............................1 Cor. 1:24

- WITNESS....................................Isaiah 55:4

- WONDERFUL..................................Isaiah 9:6

- WORD.......................................John 1:1

- WORD OF GOD...................Revelation 19:13

- YAH...........Isaiah 12:2(kjv),Psalm 68:4(nkjv)

www.ingramcontent.com/pod-product-compliance
Lightning Source LLC
Chambersburg PA
CBHW020508040426
42331CB00042BA/93